HYDROPONICS GARDENING:

THE ULTIMATE BEGINNER'S GUIDE TO LEARN HOW TO BUILD AN AFFORDABLE HYDROPONIC SYSTEM AND GROW VEGETABLES, FRUIT AND HERBS WITHOUT SOIL AT HOME

WRITTEN BY:

SAM WILLIAM GROSS

Table of Contents

Introduction

If you're a gardener, you've experienced the joy of planting and harvesting food for the table. Me? I love the beginning and the end...but not so much the middle. Endless regular watering and fertilizing, weed pulling, pest control and manicuring the garden.

Water is the essential ingredient of all life, and it has an especially vital role in the life of plants. Water provides the transport of nutrients and energy (salts and sugars) like a reliable vehicle that to the cells within a plant.

The nutrient solution that you will supply is generally provided through a human-made embedded system. This gives rise to the benefit of avoiding the evaporation that occurs in soil. In other words, we're ensuring that this nutrient-rich water is always available to our plants when they require it. Whether you know it or not, you've likely already practiced simple hydroponics by putting flowers in a vase and adding a ready-made nutrient solution.

Hydroponics is consistently growing in popularity in the modern world, from backyard ventures to hydroponic applications on space stations! Humans continue to explore the possibility of living on other planets while hydroponics play a key role in being able to provide nutrition. On a more fundamental level, hydroponics offers an affordable means of producing food for low-income areas of the world and the popularity of growing hydroponically as a hobby has gained a fair deal of popularity over recent decades.

Hydroponics is a process where plants are grown in sand, liquid or gravel with the further addition of nutrients but without soil. The word Hydroponic is got from Latin and means working water. In simple words, it is a system where plants are grown in the absence of soil. Many people assume that hydroponics is a system where these plants will be made to grow while roots are suspended in water directly minus a growing medium.

In hydroponics, a plant is grown in an environment that is inert or a medium with the growing conditions balanced. For example, the nutrient solution's pH is balanced so that the roots receive it in a form that highly soluble. In this way, the plant does not have to strain in trying to get all the nutrients that it requires. In this kind of system, a plant's exerts minimal effort in absorbing the food vis-à-vis a case scenario where a plant has to get it nutrients directly from the soil. It is a well-researched and applicable system where the organic soil that is rich in nutrients is used. It also uses other nutrients that are of high quality in getting the best results. The excess energy that could be used in absorbing nutrients by the plants is now used in the promotion of vegetative growth, flowering and even fruit production. Little wonder, it is a system that is enhancing food security in the nations of the world. Great leaps in technology have allowed plants to grow without soil. However, this unique way of planting that is rapidly becoming popular has been around for decades.

Chapter 1. What Is Hydroponics Gardening?

History and Definition of Hydroponics

Hydroponics simply means working water ("hydro" means "water" and "ponos" signifies "labor"). Many distinct civilizations have used hydroponic growing techniques: hanging gardens of Babylon, the floating gardens of the Aztecs of Mexico and people of the Chinese are cases of the 'Hydroponic' culture.

Hydroponics is of course a new way of growing plants. But giant strides have been created through the past few years in this innovative field of agriculture. Through the past century, both scientists and horticulturists have experimented with various techniques of hydroponics. Among the possible uses of hydroponics that drove research was for growing fresh produce in nonarable regions of the Earth.

It's a simple actuality that some individuals can't grow in the soil within their place (if there's any soil in it at all). This application of hydroponics was analyzed during World War II. Troops stationed on the Pacific nonarable islands were provided with locally fresh produce grown in based hydroponic systems.

Hydroponics was integrated to the space program. As NASA believed the practicalities of finding a society on a different plant or the planet's moon, hydroponics readily fit into their sustainability aims. This study is continuing. However, by the 1970s, it was not only analysts and scientists who had been included in hydroponics. Traditional farmers and keen hobbyists started to be drawn to the virtues of hydroponic growing. Some of the positive aspects of hydroponics comprise:

- The ability to create higher yields than traditional, soil-based agriculture

- Letting food be grown and eaten in regions of the world that may not support plants in the soil

- Eliminating the requirement for massive pesticide usage (considering most insects reside in the soil), effectively making our soil, air, food, and water cleaner

Commercial growers are now flocking to hydroponics like never before. The ideals enclosing these climbing techniques touch on subjects that most men and women care about, like helping end world hunger and also making the world cleaner.

Besides the extensive research that's happening, everyday folks from all around the world are constructing (or buying) their particular systems to grow great-tasting, fresh food to their loved one's members and friends. Educators are realizing that the remarkable software that hydroponics could have in the classroom.

Hydroponic Gardening is the method where crops can grow without soil. Using hydroponics to grow plants can be good for many growers, as it enables plants to be grown much faster and most times with less difficulties.

Plants are grown in a solution made up of water and dissolved nutrients necessary for the specific plant. There are lots of hydroponics systems and techniques which are utilized in growing plants that are now booming.

The different kinds of hydroponics systems and techniques include the aeroponics, nutrient film technique (or NFT), and the aeration technique.

With the aeroponics techniques, plants are fastened utilizing rigid pipes, films, or screens. The nutrients are circulated to the plants' water source and the plants' roots are suspended inside the water. The plant subsequently obtains its food nutrients directly from the water or by an air mist sprayed directly onto the plant's roots.

Hydroponic gardening also requires the use of a growing media. Various mediums may be utilized which have to keep the roots abundantly moist. They need to also be in a position to support the plant's roots. These are the best media to date: enlarged clay, perlite, Styrofoam, lavender, rockwool, vermiculite, and pea gravel.

Many types plants which could be increased in a hydroponics system. Some plants will grow much better in a hydroponics system than many others, however, a number of the very popular are carrot, tomatoes, cucumbers, herbs, watercress, and also several other edible plants.

Tree seedlings and blossoms may also be grown using hydroponics. Hydroponic greenhouses are generating countless plant seedlings each year. These are subsequently transplanted and grown in other places where they're planted into soil.

If you are only a beginner at hydroponic gardening, you may undoubtedly be more concerned with the level of your plants and the faster rate of expansion. Hydroponically grown plants will grow and grow faster and give you an earlier harvest of vegetable plants.

There are many advantages to growing your plants in a hydroponics system. Hydroponic gardening does not call for a fertile farmland or even a massive water source for growing crops. Vegetable and plants can be grown year-round. Hydroponic plants and vegetables can be grown in just about any small area, or a cellar, or even a flat balcony.

The hydroponic systems need less space since the plant's roots do not need to propagate and hunt for water and food. The smaller area requirement creates hydroponic gardening ideal for limited space house gardeners.

Hydroponic plants can likewise be grown in nurseries and greenhouses. The advantage of growing these crops with soil in a sterile medium comprises not needing to eliminate weeds or coping with soil-borne insects and diseases. And because most of the nutrients essential for the plant are easily accessible for this, the plant is more obviously fitter compared to plants grown in soil.

The best advantage to hydroponic gardening is your capacity to automate the hydroponics system with sockets and remote monitoring equipment. This lessens the time it requires to keep the crops and the growing air. Additionally, it enables the grower to leave their method for lengthy lengths of time without worrying about watering the plants.

Hydroponic growing without using soil isn't straightforward, but with time it will get to be very simple and regular. Hydroponics gives the benefit of several methods which may be beneficial to your crops and create a richer and healthy plant.

How is Hydroponic Gardening Different from Regular Gardening?

When growing via hydroponics, you will find a huge range of growing mediums which might be utilized. The mediums include substances such as perlite, vermiculite, coconut fiber, gravel, sand, or some variety of different substances. Even air might be utilized as a hydroponic growing medium.

Each of the nutrition requirements comes in the nutrient solution, normally mixing fertilizer and water. Hydroponic fertilizer and fertilizer meant for usage in soil (regular fertilizer) include the three major nutrients. These nutrients are nitrogen, phosphorus, as well as potassium. The most important difference between hydroponic fertilizer and soil fertilizer is the fact that hydroponic gardening fertilizers include the appropriate amounts of each one of the vital micro-nutrients that fertilizers don't include. The crops are expected to discover these components in the soil.

Issues may arise for the plants if some or all the micro-nutrients aren't found in the soil or have been depleted by sequential or excess plantings. Hydroponic gardening fertilizers are often in a purer form compared to the regular fertilizers, so they're more secure and water-soluble.

Organic fertilizers are typically different than the hydroponic fertilizers or even the soil fertilizers in the way they deliver nourishment to plants. The organic fertilizers trust the action of microbes and bacteria to help divide the material into its fundamental elements so the plants can quickly use it. Hydroponic and regular fertilizers subsequently provide for the plants using these components.

Another difference between hydroponic and normal gardening is that growing hydroponics can be extremely complex. Hydroponics are controlled with sensors and computers that help control everything from watering cycles to nutrient power, and the total amount of light the plants receive. But hydroponics may also be rather straightforward. The normal home hydroponic system generally contains a couple of essential components, such as a growing menu, a reservoir, a timer controlled submersible pump to water the crops, along with an air pump to oxygenate the nutrient solution. Lighting is, of course, also needed to assist the hydroponic garden to grow.

Additionally, there are micro-nutrients which are needed for healthy plant growth. All these micro-nutrients include sulfur, calcium, magnesium, boron, cobalt, iron, copper, manganese, magnesium, and molybdenum. These nutrients are the vital components plants need in tiny quantities. Plants will probably become ill with no trace components and also will grow all kinds of issues if that nutrient is lost.

The lack of micro-nutrients in food plants can signify a deficiency of nutrition in the food. This is going to lead to the food not being as healthy as it might be and possibly lead folks to grow health issues as a result of deficiency of the vital elements. Any hydroponic gardener should use a good quality hydroponic fertilizer when they're growing plants with hydroponics.

It's also vital that the pH is regulated in both growing via hydroponics and in the soil. Plants lose the capability to consume unique nutrients once the pH varies. The pH needs to be monitored throughout the whole growth cycle of these plants to keep up the utmost healthy uptake of nutrients. The pH of the nutrient solution can influence how well each component can pass through the main cell wall to nourish the plant. When the gardener has correctly calibrated the proper concentrations and the pH of the solution, they can normally assume it'll remain steady barring any unexpected root disease.

Advantages of Hydroponic Gardening

So, have you decided to grow a garden this season? Well, prior to going out and spending a great deal of money unnecessarily, you ought to have a peek at the benefits of hydroponic gardening. Hydroponic gardening is garden work at its very best. There's almost little to no soil involved with hydroponic growing. Hydroponic gardening is the usage of light and water to grow fruits and vegetables.

Hydroponic growing means less time and not as much money wasted on unnecessary substances. You don't have to spend money on pesticides and fertilizers. Nor would you spend hours weeding and tilling the ground. Hydroponic gardening is quite valuable because the yields on plants are much higher and the crops will normally generate richer, brighter, and more fruits.

To begin your personal hydroponic garden, you have to choose where you'll settle your crops. The hydroponic growth of crops generally implies that you need a nice quantity of room to enable the crops to grow. Many men and women use a greenhouse. Hydroponic growth of crops is quite straightforward and virtually everyone can get it done.

All you will need is to do just a bit of research, particularly if you're just beginning. Ask questions from those that you know who are in gardening. Learn what sort of nutrients that your plants will require. Hydroponic nutrients are often more concentrated due to the simple fact they have to get added into the plants and their growing environment. It's advisable if you discover a combination solution that will offer all the nutrients required for the plants to grow.

Hydroponic gardening can grow your veggies and fruits throughout the year. This way it is possible to control not merely the water and light, but also the number of pests which will impact the return of these plants. When growing a garden outside, you need to be ready to eliminate some of your harvest yield as a result of pests, the weather, along with other aspects. But with hydroponic growing, you are able to remove the majority of these variables.

You might even be able to guarantee the quantity of hydroponic nutrients your plants need. By utilizing hydroponic nutrients, you can control the strength of their main systems and restrain the flowering potential of your crops. Various kinds of hydroponic nutrients may promote your plants to make more blossoms, which then provide more fruit in crops like the tomato plant. Other kinds of hydroponic nutrients boost the dimensions and foliage of these plants. Hydroponic nutrients are essentially plant food. This is as vital to the plant's growth as light and water.

Chapter 2. Hydroponics Vs Soil Gardening

Both hydroponic and soil gardening methods have their advantages and disadvantages, you will discover that not all plants are suitable for hydroponic systems. However, a surprising number are, including many that you would not think could be grown without soil, such as potatoes and carrots.

Areas Where Hydroponic Gardening is Better Than Soil Gardening

Hydroponics save space

Hydroponics take up very little space, and you can grow an indoor hydroponic system in your room. Besides, the absence of soil means root systems are short, so you can grow plants closer together and save space.

Weather free growing

The weather can be the biggest hindrance to growing anything outside. In a hydroponic system, you have full control over the environment and are growing indoors, so there is no weather to upset your growing plans!

Lower water use

Growing in soil is surprisingly water inefficient, so in an area where water is expensive or scarce it is very costly to grow vegetables. However, a hydroponic system, despite being made up mainly of water, using significantly less water than growing in soil because it is more efficient in its use of water.

Fewer pests

Have you ever lost your crop to pests? Had caterpillars devoured your cauliflower? Pests are a significant problem when growing outside and mean either companion planting, using pesticide, or accepting you will lose a portion of your crop. Hydroponic plants are grown indoors in an enclosed environment, so the chances of pests are meager. Of course, there is the chance that you will find the occasional pest, but as you are regularly checking the system, you tend to spot any pest problems very early on before they cause much damage.

Fewer diseases

It is very frustrating to lose your entire crop because of a disease. Although you can spray for many conditions, there are just as many for which there is no treatment. As you are growing indoors, diseases are very uncommon. Practicing proper hygiene and quarantining new plants before introducing them to the system will help to reduce the risk of illness to virtually zero.

Fewer artificial chemicals

Although there is a significant movement away from the use of chemicals in gardening, they are still introduced into your garden through the wind and rain. However, some gardeners will use pesticides and artificial fertilizers. Growing hydroponically, you use far fewer chemicals, which is a huge benefit for many gardeners.

No digging

A distaste of many gardeners is the need to dig over the soil, hence the popularity of systems such as the no-dig system involving layering compost and cardboard. There is no digging involved in hydroponic gardening, as there is no soil.

Rapid maturing crops

When you grow plants hydroponically, they mature far faster than if they are grown in soil or even in a greenhouse. Typically, plants will develop in three-quarters of the usual growing time, but some can mature in up to half the time.

Reliable & predictable yields

Growing hydroponically produces very reliable yields because you are not reliant on the vagrancies of the weather. Yields are typically much higher because of the consistent growing conditions, producing up to double the yield.

Lower labor requirement

Because there is less work involved, you just check the pH and nutrient levels regularly, there is a lot less labor involved.

Higher nutritional content

Scientific analysis of hydroponically grown vegetables has shown that they contain up to 50% more vitamins and minerals than vegetables grown in soil. Obviously, this means some health benefits and is a big advantage for many growers.

Hydroponics uses less water

When grown via a hydroponic system, the plants need less water. When you water plants that are in the soil, often the water seeps into the ground, and some water also gets evaporated. But the hydroponic system is much more water-efficient, and you use 70 to 80% less water.

Hydroponics systems lower, pests, weeds, and diseases

With traditional soil planting the risk of pests, weeds, and diseases increases; but a hydroponic system deals with this problem almost completely.

Hydroponic systems grow plants faster

Hydroponic systems grow plants twice as fast as traditional methods, which means you get more harvests every year. The growing cycle is much more efficient because the plants get everything it needs.

Hydroponics let you adjust nutrient content for different plants

Hydroponics allows you to tweak and adapt nutrients for every plant.

Areas Where Soil Gardening is Better

Lower initial cost

The initial cost of hydroponics can be quite expensive. But soil gardening has a lower initial price.

No need to use electricity

A light source is needed in several hydroponic gardening techniques. Also, some systems use power to aerate the roots.

Less risk of bacteria and mold growth

In a hydroponics system, plants grow in a very moist environment. If precautions are not taken, then there is a susceptible risk of mold and bacteria growth.

Now you know the main differences between the traditional soil growing method and the hydroponics system.

Chapter 3. How It Works?

Hydroponics works primarily because plants do not actually need soil at all—they need the nutrients that come out of the soil. When you can get those nutrients from the soil and saturate them into water, you instead allow for the entire system to be effective at growing with ease. Instead of the mess from soil, you wind up with a water solution that can be provided to the plant, saving it energy at the end of the day.

Plants naturally have to branch out their roots in order to get the energy that they need for their systems. When they do not have easy access to doing so, they begin to struggle to produce the leaves and fruit that is atop them. The roots are the foragers, so to speak—they pull in crucial elements to plant growth to allow for it to process. Without the roots, you cannot have the plant. The leaves are also important, as they allow for the absorption of the sunlight that works to aid in the processing of the water and carbon dioxide into the glucose that the plants need. However, without the roots to pull in the important nutrients, there can be no photosynthesis in the first place, leading to a system in which the plants cannot grow properly.

Plants have very specific requirements if they want to be able to grow effectively. These requirements are quite simple: They need light from the sun, carbon dioxide, and water. With those three elements, they take create glucose, with a byproduct of oxygen as well. This occurs through the process of photosynthesis, which works with the following equation:

Light + 6CO2 + 6H2O ------> C6H12O6 + 6O2

With that equation in mind, you can see that ultimately, the plant will take in the light from the sun in the leaves. This allows for six distinct carbon dioxide molecules and six oxygen molecules to be broken down and turned into a single glucose molecule and six oxygen molecules. When this happens, the plant now has its source of energy. Like all plants and animals, plants require glucose for energy. This is the same source of energy that humans use to provide energy to the body for respiration and other processes.

If you take a close look at that equation, you see that there is nothing in it that requires soil. While you can mix water into soil, it is not an inherent part of the soil itself. Now, let's consider the elements and nutrients that plants need:

1.Nitrogen

2.Phosphorus

3.Potassium

4.Magnesium

5.Sulfur

6.Calcium

All of these are needed in varying degrees for different purposes for the plant to grow and thrive. Again, these are very important, but do you see anything that is specific to soil?

The root system of plants is meant to go looking for those various elements, but at the end of the day, they are not necessarily a part of the soil. The plant does not actually need any soil if it can get these elements elsewhere, which is precisely why hydroponics works as a method to grow in the first place.

In a hydroponic garden, you are setting everything up for the plant. You ensure that the plant will have enough water to grow, and you also ensure that the water will be saturated with the necessary nutrients to grow. You make sure that the system is properly able to support itself in an inert medium. You make sure that the plant is going to have enough light presented to it. You are essentially going to make sure that everything is as readily available as possible for the plant to thrive. When you can do this, your plants will grow quickly and readily.

When you are using a hydroponic system, you are going to go through various steps to complete the process, and these are largely dependent on the system that you have chosen for the process. Some will require that you pay close attention to the plant itself. Others will require that you can set up timers to run the system for you. Overall, however, you will have to follow these steps to ensure that your system, no matter what kind of system it is, will work properly.

Step 1: Assembly

The first step is making sure that you know what you intend to grow in the first place. In particular, you are going to need to set up a system with regard to the particular system that you are using. This means that you will need to figure out the instructions for your system and follow them closely to ensure that the system itself is put together properly. If you are building one yourself with a guide, you will want to make sure that it is at least functional and that you are not going to find that you lose any of your nutrients.

When you are trying to choose out which system is right for you, you have many different considerations to make. You need to figure out how much money you are willing to spend and how much time you are willing to spend working on the system as you grow.

Step 2: Selecting your plants

You will want to ensure that the system that you have chosen is going to properly work for the plants before you begin to try to cultivate them. If the plants are not properly suited to the particular method that you are going to be using, then you may want to either choose a new plant or a new method. In particular, for a beginner, lettuce is perhaps one of the easiest to cultivate just due to the needs that it has in the first place. They are very easy to meet when you have a system that is entirely hooked up to the water, and you are constantly allowing your system to run.

Selecting the lighting, nutrients, and scheduling

With the plants in mind, you must ensure that you are able to provide the nutrients that they will require. This means that you will need to do a bit of research on the specific variant of the plant that you are growing. If you have a variant that has specific needs compared to more common strains of that particular plant, you will want to guarantee that you can accommodate, and because of that, you will need to pay close attention to those needs.

Certain strains of plants may also have varying lighting requirements and stricter requirements for nutrients and water. You will want to make sure that you know everything about your plant to set it up with the system that is going to work properly for it. If you cannot guarantee this, you run the risk of the whole system failing entirely or your plant not producing much or quality products. A common issue that people can run into is that their produce winds up being flavorless in general, and that is a problem for many people. They want their produce to have plenty of flavor—that is why they are growing it at home! When they undernourish the plant, however, they run the risk of it simply never developing properly in the first place.

Mixing the nutrients

After you know what you will need for your plants, you will then be able to process the nutritional content that it requires. This is done through the use of either buying the mixture at the store or trying to balance it yourself. The mixture must then be added to your reservoir to allow it to be processed through your system.

Add the plants

After your nutrients are all mixed up and processed, and your system is ready to go, you can begin to plant everything where it belongs. Make sure that you always remember to pay attention to the requirements for space and for lighting for them. While most of the time, you do not need as much space in your system when growing hydroponically, there are still requirements for the space that you will be using. You will need to give your plants the proper amount of space that they will need in order to properly stretch out their leaves to grow accordingly. If you cannot do this, they may run the risk of smothering themselves out and dying off before you had a chance to really cultivate them at all.

Monitor the system regularly

At this point, your job is going to be to make sure that your system is running as it should be. At first, you may want to check on it two to three times a day—this is because if you leave it too long without looking at it, you run the risk of missing if and when it fails. For the first few weeks, you should regularly make it a point to check all piping, make sure that water is running, and ensure that ultimately, it all works properly. If you can do this, you will be able to catch any problems nearly immediately.

You will find that you can check it a bit less regularly, but you are still going to want to be inspecting often. When your system fails you and you have a system that relies on electricity to process everything, you run the risk of taking far too long to make sure that everything is running properly. Your plants cannot often tolerate long periods of lacking water because they do not have the medium of soil around them, allowing them to soak up water and retain that moisture.

Check plants regularly

Finally, you will want to make sure that you are also regularly checking over your plants for growth and signs of illness or pests. When you do this, you ensure that you are protecting your system. You can make sure that you catch any signs that the nutritional balance is off or that your plants are not growing the way that they should be. You can see whether you are suffering from some sort of infestation that will require treatment, or you can catch on to any other problems that may arise. All of this is critically important—it will allow you to figure out whether there is anything that you must change to ensure that the system runs properly.

When you go through all of these steps and make sure that everything is working just right, you then get the end result—you discover that your system has processed everything, and as a result, you get to harvest everything that is there. You will get to reap the benefits of your efforts. You will be able to pick up everything that you have grown and begin to consume it on your own. You should find that you get larger and quicker yields with your hydroponic system, but if you are not, you may need to add in some troubleshooting to the mix as well. You are going to want to find these mistakes that are being made so you can really maximize the output of your systems and ensure that ultimately, you are going to find that you can eventually max out to getting several harvests from a single plant and harvesting many more units than you would have if you had grown traditionally. Due to the fact that the growing time is generally shorter with a hydroponic setup, you usually get to see the added benefit of getting more cycles of growth within a single growing season, meaning that the end output is much better than you normally would see.

Chapter 4. Different Types of Hydroponics Systems

1. The Drip System

Drip systems are one of the most broadly utilized types of hydroponic systems around the globe, both for home producers just as business cultivators the same. That is for the most part since it's a simple idea and necessities scarcely any parts, however yet it's an adaptable and compelling type of hydroponic system. Despite the fact that it's a simple idea, it won't restrict your creative mind when fabricating your own systems. The manner in which a drip system works is much the same as it sounds; you just drip nutrient arrangement on the plant's roots to keep them clammy.

Hydroponic drip systems can, without much of a stretch, be structured from numerous points of view, just as from little to enormous systems. Be that as it may, their particularly valuable for bigger plants that take a great deal of root space. That is on the grounds that you needn't bother with huge volumes of water to flood the system, and the drip lines are anything but difficult to run over longer spaces. Just as when utilizing a bigger measure of developing media for bigger plants, more developing media holds more dampness than littler sums, and that is especially helpful to huge plants since it's all the more lenient to the plants. Pardoning implying that the plants aren't as sensitive to watering times, so they don't pressure immediately on the off chance that they don't get watered on schedule for some explanation.

2. Ebb and Flow (Flood and Drain) System

Ebb and Flow - (also called Flood and Drain system) System.

These Flood and Drain systems are famous for home hydroponic producers for some reason. Other than how simple they are for anybody to fabricate, you can utilize practically any materials you have laying around to construct them with, so you don't have to go through a lot of cash to develop plants hydroponically.

At the point when the water filling/flooding, the system arrives at the overflow tube tallness, it depletes down to the supply where it recycles back through the system once more. The overflow tube sets the water level tallness in the flood and channel system, just as ensures the water (nutrient arrangement) doesn't spill out the highest point of the system while the siphon is on. At the point when the siphon closes off, the water guides down into the supply through the siphon (depleting the system).

What you need to construct a Flood and Drain system:

•	A compartment for the plant's underlying foundations to develop in.

•	A compartment (store) to hold the nutrient arrangement.

•	A submersible wellspring/lake siphon.

- A light clock to kill the siphon on and.

- Some tubing to run from the siphon in the supply to the system to be flooded.

- An overflow tube set to the tallness you need the water level.

- Growing mechanism or something to that effect.

3. Nutrient Film Techniques

In nutrient film technology, some roots of the plant are in the nutrient solution, while large parts are only in the air. The plant is thus ideally supplied with the optimal mixture of nutrients and oxygen. As soon as young plants have formed sufficiently long roots, they are put into the plant tube (gully, canal) together with the netting and substrate. In this circulatory system, the nutrient solution is pumped from the reservoir into the canal. The nutrient solution then flows in a thin film down the slightly angled channel into the return flow that flows back to the source container. The nft system is perceived as pleasantly easy and often used commercially. However, there are some principles to be followed for the growth of the plants to succeed.

Shape

The usual height for the canal is 4 - 5 cm. The roots do not grow in-depth but in width. The width is determined depending on the expected root mass.

Gradient

A gradient of 1:16 is recommended. This means that for a 16 at the long gully, the height difference is 1 cm. Theoretically, the gradient could be 1: 100 cm. In practice, however, then congestion forms, which contradict the principle of the system, only to produce a film of nutrient solution.

Throughput

For 10 cm wide channels, a throughput of 0.5 l per minute is recommended for wide channels 2 l. The gradient also affects the thickness of the film. The film should be neither too deep nor too shallow.

Length

The length of the channel from the inlet of the nutrient solution to its outflow is limited. If the canal is too long, the supply of nutrients and oxygen for all plants can no longer be maintained. The length of the gully depends on the gradient and throughput. As a rule of thumb, it should not be more than 10 to 15 meters, or it should be pumped after this length at the latest fresh nutrient solution.

4. Deep Water Culture System (Dwc)

Deep water culture is a cultivation method in which the plants are kept floating in the nutrient solution, and the roots are suspended directly in the nutrient solution.

The deep-water culture is an active hydroponic system in which the roots of the plant are suspended in a nutrient solution. Thus, the plant is always supplied with water and nutrients.

The plants are stuck in net pots and are fixed with a substrate.

The mesh pots can be placed over the water surface in two ways: either you drill holes in the lid of the water reservoir, or you put the pigtails in a floating platform.

Three advantages make a deep-water culture so popular:

- Low maintenance

- Fast and easy to build

- Very efficient and profitable

What you need to assemble a Water Culture system:

- Aquarium vacuum apparatus

- The Baskets, pots, and the cups to hold the plants

- Growing media

- Container to hold the nutrient arrangement (supply)

- Air stones (or soaker hose) to make the little air pockets

- Airline/hose

Recirculating

Hydroponic systems are used very often and commercially under the hydroponic system. If one uses the technique on a larger scale, one usually uses several targets and one central source reservoir. That's how you save air stones. However, then the roots are no longer supplied directly with air bubbles, but only with oxygen dissolved in water from the central nutrient tank. Thus, increasing the amount of dissolved oxygen, the target container is flooded continuously, and by overflow water flowing to the central reservoir cascading led back. By refluxing waterfalls into the source container, additional oxygen is taken. The deeper the waterfalls, the more oxygen is supplied. Since the water in the destination container always overflows, there must be no amount of water controlled, but only in the source container. So, there is only one place where most parameters such as ph, nutrient solution concentration, water temperature, oxygen content, must be monitored and monitored.

5. Aeroponics

While the idea of the aeroponic system is very basic, it's really the most specialized of every one of the 6 types of hydroponic systems. However, it's still genuinely simple to construct your own essential aeroponic system, and a ton of home growers like growing in them too, and even get great outcomes utilizing this type of hydroponic system.

There are a couple of setbacks to aeroponic systems too. Other than being more costly to fabricate. The sir/sprinkler heads can stop up from work of the broke down mineral components in the nutrient arrangement. So, try to have additional items close by to swap out when they do obstruct while you clean them. Additionally, because the plants establish are hanging in mid-air by the structure in aeroponic systems, the plant's roots are considerably more defenseless against drying out if there is any break in the watering cycle. Therefore, even any brief force blackout (under any circumstances) could make your plants bite the dust significantly more rapidly than some other type of hydroponic system. Additionally, there's a decreased edge for blunder with the nutrient levels in aeroponic systems, particularly the genuine high weight systems.

What you'll have to manufacture your own fundamental Aeroponic system:

- Container to hold the nutrient arrangement (a repository).

- Submersible wellspring/lake siphon.

- Tubing to disseminate water from the supply siphon to the mister heads   in the growing chamber.

- Enclosed growing chamber for the root zone.

- Mister/sprinkler heads.

- Watertight compartment for the growing chamber where the plant's root systems will be.

- Tubing to restore the overabundance nutrient arrangement back to the store.

- Timer (ideally a cycle clock) to kill on and the siphon.

How the aeroponic system works is a genuinely simple idea. First, the motivation behind the roots hangs in mid-air is so they can get the most extreme measure of oxygen that they can get. The high volume of oxygen the roots get permits the designs to grow quicker than they would something else, and the primary advantage to this type of hydroponic system.

Second, there is regularly no growing media is utilized, uncovering all the plant's roots. The plants are suspended either by little bushels or shut cell froth plugs that pack around the plant's stem. These crates or froth connects little fit openings at the highest point of the growing chamber. The roots hang down inside the growing chamber where they get splashed with a nutrient arrangement from mister heads at normal short cycles. The ordinary watering cycles keep the roots wet and from drying out, just as gives the nutrients the plants need to grow.

Finally, a central point in aeroponic systems is the water bead size. Roots showered with a fine fog will grow a lot quicker, bushier, and with progressively surface, zone to assimilate nutrients and oxygen with than roots splashed with little surges of water like from little sprinkler heads. That converts into the plant shelter growing all the more quickly also. Aeroponic system types are sorted by the water bead size.

6. Wick System

This is by far the easiest of all of the systems to build. Typically, this system only needs four components and you can build it out of things that you have lying around. The four components that you need include a container or containers for the plants to grow in a growing medium or suitable substrate, a reservoir for the water and nutrient solution to flow through, and a wick system.

The growing containers are positioned above the reservoir and the wick systems are positioned in such a way that they will absorb the nutrient solution and draw this up, releasing it to where the plant root system is, making it available to the plants. This method works on the same principle that a wick would draw oil to fuel an oil lamp. This system is commonly referred to as being a passive system (meaning that you don't need any pumps and other working equipment for it to work).

This is not to say that you can't make use of a pump or other forms of aerating the water, as a matter of fact, this is very often the option that most hydroponic growers will adopt.

Another reason for choosing the wick system is that it is the most environmentally friendly of all systems. You don't need electricity when using this system (if you are not going to attach a pump), your plants can be placed in a position where they can get enough natural light for them to grow. This wick system also uses much less water and nutrients than any of the other systems.

A major reason for this method being chosen for beginners is that it is extremely simple to start with and is fairly maintenance free - the only major work that needs to be done is to refill the nutrient solution on a regular basis and to flush the system, when necessary. This system is best for plants that aren't going to bear fruit - lettuce and herbs are ideal.

Chapter 5.How to Start Your Hydroponics Garden

Now that we know the different kinds of hydroponic setups that are available to us, it is time to see how they are built. We will be looking at three of the different setups, those most suited for beginners. This means that the system you choose should be the one that fits your desires.

While there are many sites and businesses out there that will sell you hydroponic kits, it can be very easy to make them ourselves. This isn't to say there is no value in store-bought kits. But before we go spending a lot of money, a DIY setup can be a great way to get a handle on the basics of setting up a hydroponic garden. Once we know what we are doing, we can then start to add on all sorts of gears and gizmos to personalize and level up our gardens. But we have to start somewhere, and DIY is a great place to kick off from.

Drip system

For this system, we're going to look at one of the easy-to-build drip systems. This one uses buckets in which to grow the plants which still receive their nutrient-rich water through a series of tubes. In order to accomplish this design, there are three key areas which we need to build: the buckets, the reservoir and the tubing. We will look at what it takes to make a single plant setup, but we'll see how easy it is to adapt the system to include more.

Start with your bucket. For our purposes, we'll begin with a five-gallon bucket, but you can increase or decrease the size as necessary. The first thing we do is flip the bucket upside down so that we can get at the bottom easily. We're looking to get the drain into place so that any water dripped into the system will be recycled back into the reservoir. To do this we will be using a thru-hole fitting. These little guys are used in all sorts of different fields and you can easily pick one up for a dollar or two at any hardware store.

Place the thru hole on the bottom of the bucket, thread side making contact, and trace around it. This should give you a small little circle on the bottom of your buckets. We want this circle to be closer to the edge than to the middle, as we want our bucket to be able to sit comfortably on an elevated surface. With that in place, cut out the circle you have traced and insert the thru hole into the bucket. Tighten the thru hole in place. Your bucket now has a drain installed. Take a filter of some sort, can be a furnace filter or any kind really, and cut enough out to place over the thru hole inside the bucket. This helps to keep only water draining and not our growing medium.

We should also paint our buckets. We can double up this task and paint our reservoirs at the same time. Use a black paint on the outside of the bucket in order to block light from entering which would lead to algae growth. With the buckets painted black, they are going to attract a lot of heat which would raise the temperature of our water and could prove to be a real pain in the long run. For this reason, it is suggested that you use a coat or two of white paint over the black paint so as to reflect the light rather than absorb it.

We're going to do a similar design when it comes to our reservoir, but the key difference is the hole we cut will be in the top and not in the bottom. Having painted the reservoir black and then white, we will cut a hole in the top of it through which we can feed the cording for our pump and for the hoses. That's all that the reservoir takes.

But in order to make this work from here, we need to connect them using tubing. Connect the tube to the hose and feed it up to the bucket. You can use glue, tape, or whatever method you prefer in order to keep the tube in place to feed your plants. One effective way is to create a loop that sits inside the inside of the bucket, poke a ton of little holes in it and then connect that tube to your main tube. That way water would flow up through the main tube, connect to the inner bucket tube and it would work like a mini sprinkler system. This way makes sure that the water is spread around the bucket and not confined to a single area.

With the feeder tube in place, we then need to attach the draining tube. This is as easy as hooking our tubing up to the thru hole we inserted and running it back down into the reservoir. It is important that we keep our grow bucket elevated above the reservoir so that gravity can do its trick.

In order to make sure that we aren't drowning our plants, it's important that we get a digital timer and hook it up so that we aren't pumping water at all times. We'll want to get a timer that allows us to set many different times rather than just one time because we want our system to turn off and on several times a day rather than just once. We need to do this in order to make sure that our plants are getting the right amount of nutrients.

So that is how you set up a single bucket drip system. If you want to expand the system, it is actually very easy. Let's say that you wanted to do four buckets instead of just one. You take those buckets and you give them their thru holes and a paint job all the same. The major difference between running a single bucket setup and a four-bucket setup is the tubing. Rather than running a single tube from our reservoir to our bucket, we are going to instead use T-connectors.

Take the tubing that runs out of the reservoir and connect it into a T-connector. This will give you a tube that looks like a T-corner like we see on the roads. Instead of being a single tube with one ending, you now have two tubes each with their own ending. This would allow us to use a two-bucket setup. However, we choose a four-bucket setup for this example. This means that we have to take each of those tubes and again run them into a T-connector. Now each side gets split into two and we have four ends, one for each of our buckets and we have quadrupled the size of our grow operation.

With all the building in place, we then just have to pack in our buckets. Some rocks at the bottom of each bucket can serve to help weigh them down but it's not absolutely needed. This is more a precaution, though it is one that is recommended. Over the rocks, you pack in your growing medium and then you get your plants in there.

Wicking system

Wicking is simply the use of a wick able material going from our reservoir to our grow tray. This can be rope, felt, string; whatever material you can easily get your hands on for the wicking will work.

Again, we are going to paint the reservoir black and then cover it in a coat of white paint to prevent it from supporting algae or growing too hot. We are then going to cut or drill very small holes in the cover of the reservoir through which we will thread our wicks.

Our grow trays are going to be filled with a medium that is particularly well-suited to wicking such as perlite or coco coir. But before we fill them up, we first want to cut or drill tiny holes into the bottom of the tray as we did to the cover of the reservoir. These will be roughly the same size because they are how the wick gets the nutrients to the plants.

Ultimately, we have our wicks almost entirely submerged in the water. They are then fed up and nested in the growing tray very close to the plants. We can use more than one wick per plant depending on the plant's particular water and nutrient needs.

As far as set up, that's really it. We place our plants into the grow tray, and we watch how they grow. However, there are some tips and tricks that will make a more successful wicking system. We might consider using an air pump to aerate the water so that our plants are able to get more oxygen as this will help them to grow faster. Another thing we will want to consider is keeping the grow tray closer to the reservoir with a wicking system than we would with a drip system. This is because the nutrients aren't pumped to our plants in this system but have to rely on what is called capillary action (aka, wicking). Having our wicks shorter means, they can more easily provide. The distance between our wicks and the grow tray is one way of doing this. Another is making sure that the level of the water in our reservoir is high, as this shortens the distance as well.

Deep water culture

Since a deep-water culture uses deep water (it's there in the name, after all), we will be using a five-gallon bucket because of the depth that it gives us. While some people refer to any system of plants floating on the water as a deep-water system, we need to have ten plus inches of water for it to be considered deep. We could grow a small plant in a small culture, and have it been equivalent in ratios to that of a deep-water culture, but it still wouldn't be proper to call it such.

The first thing that we are going to do, surprise, is paint our bucket black and then white. Slightly underneath the lid, we are also going to cut a little hole for the tubing of our air pump so that we can oxygenate the water.

Because a deep-water culture works by having the roots of the plant soaking in the water, we need to design a setup so that our plants can bath. To do this, we can go out and buy what is called a plant basket. This is a basket that looks like your typical plant pot but instead, it has a ton of holes through the lower half. Alternatively, we can also just take a plant pot and then cut, drill or solder holes into it. This is going to be our grow tray.

We'll be filling our grow tray up with our desired growing medium and the plant that we want to raise but first, we need to integrate it into the system. To do this we will be cutting a hole in the lid of our five-gallon bucket. At this point, it is best to cut a smaller hole and make it larger as needed rather than start with a large hole. This is because it is far easier to increase the size of the hole than it is to block it back up. If we make our hole too big, our grow tray will just fall into the bucket and we will need to get another lid and try all over again. Our goal is for the lower half of the pot to fit into the hole and be held in place by the pot's rim against the bucket's lid.

Chapter 6. Tips and Tricks to Growing Healthy Herbs, Vegetables and Fruits

Did you know that in order to get the optimum results out of the hydroponic system, you must know the right way of growing hydroponic plants so that they will yield more crops? Many individuals quickly get disappointed with hydroponic gardening, amateur growth, and as they are beginners. However, the reason for this disappointment can be one of these: -

Lack of ability- for hydroponics system you need experience, or you don't have sufficient equipment or supplies.

Unorganized- you know everything regards to hydroponic gardening, but you want to put forth the maximum effort into it.

Let's put some light on the varied hydroponic tips and tricks in below points by which you can become an expert and fulfill your dreams:

Choosing the right type of crop

In the technique of the hydroponic system, almost every plant can grow, but as a beginner, you can start with small plants by which you gain knowledge and experience.

The first step is, choose those plants which need less maintenance and nutrients. As a beginner, you can take herbs and vegetables. Therefore, growing small plants can improve your experience as well as learn new things which are best for the future when you produce other plants.

Make a proper plan

When you make up your mind to plant a specific type of crop in your hydroponic garden. Planning means knowing varied kind of nutrients which are essential for plant, various equipment, photoperiod, etc. so that you have a full overview of how it can offer better results.

Why and when to test and adjust the ph level in hydroponic plants

Every plant which you plant in your hydroponic garden only absorbs nutrient solution in the PH if the answer is in between the range of plant which you have planted. However, if the Ph is not up to the mark, then it won't matter how much your nutrient solution is, the plants will definitely suffer from malnutrition and will die after some time.

Have proper and sufficient lighting

When you search the market, you will get countless types of grow lights according to your budget. To offer the right kind of lighting to the plants, you have to gain knowledge on that which depends upon the space, the overall distance between the plants, and most crucially the budget.

The types of lighting are:

High-Intensity Discharge (HID) is suitable for extensive hydroponic gardens which have virtuous airflow and proper ventilation.

Compact Fluorescent Lights (CFL) offer good results in small rooms.

Light Emitting Lights (LED) are also best for small hydroponic gardening but they are more expensive than CFLs.

Whatever, you opt, to make sure that it will discharge light between 400 and 700 nanometers.

Having control on temperature

This is one of the essential tips of hydroponic gardening. If the temperature of the plant exceeds 85 degrees, the overall growth of the plants will stop quickly. If the gardener is using HID lights, then it becomes challenging to control the temperature.

For maintaining the accurate temperature, the gardener has to install centrifugal fans, but in some cases, the fans alone cannot solve the problem.

For this, plan hydroponic gardening when the outside temperature is 55 degrees or less. Therefore, it is possible to pull fresh air in the garden. On the other hand, you can install air conditioning.

The right type of equipment

First and foremost, one thing which you need to consider before setting up a system of the hydroponic garden is to have proper and unique tools. Like- dark area, hydroponic gardening system, an oscillating fan, TDS meter, maybe an air conditioner, a digital timer, etc.

Select an appropriate nutrient

You have to gain knowledge with regards to varied nutrients which are crucial for plant growth when you start gardening. Side by side, an individual must know about the quantity of nutrient required by diverse plants or which plant you have grown.

However, timely purchase the adequate and right equipment to check the nutrient level of the plants as per the requirement.

The health of the roots

The health of the root is essential for the overall growth of the plant. Time to time check the origins of the crop so that plants will not suffer from any damage. While offering nutrients to the plants minimizes the amount of light so that algae and fungus will not damage the roots of the crops.

Offering water to the plants

This tip is one of the crucial ones because overwatering the plants will damage the crops. In reality, the water intake of the plants depend upon the type of plants means whether it is small or large.

Crops that grow on dry season need more water than crops which grow in a humid climate. On the other hand, some plants hold moisture for a long time as compared to other plants. So, while planting a crop see whether it needs more water or less so that you can set up the water draining system.

Maintain the humidity level

Varied plants have a different level of humidity on which they can survive on their development. So, keep in mind that plants will grow faster and yield higher crops when they are given the proper level of humidity.

Airflow and ventilation should be proper

For the healthy growth of crops, airflow is the very vital part which also aids in maintaining the overall temperature of the plants. Fans and air conditioners should be installed in appropriate areas so that plants will be healthy.

Understand ph first

The understanding of PH level in plants is must get success in hydroponic gardening. Interestingly, there are meters that can take the Ph readings, but on your side, you also have to understand this. The main reason for checking the PH level of plants is that water doesn't have a proper range of Ph by which plants can die or suffer from malnutrition.

Make liberal use of your pruning shears

Any time of the day when you see something on the plant just prune it away, it can rot the full plant. The cleaner you keep your plant higher the yield.

Think about the taste of the fruits or vegetables

In this regard, which fruit or vegetable tastes excellent when it is purchased from the market or plucked from the hydroponic garden?

The main motive of doing this is there is an end number of crops that don't have a different taste. Either they are purchased from the market or plucked from the garden. Before deciding to choose the crop to plant give priority to those fruits or vegetables that taste better when they are freshly harvested from the garden.

Take care of space and type of hydroponic system

Well, it is fascinating to grow crops such as corns, melons, and squash, etc but the point is they need ample space. Make sure that you choose the right system and appropriate hydroponic kits. There are countless factors like ventilation, water, etc are crucial elements which make the hydroponic system successful.

Always plant fastest-growing, most natural cultivation, and most crucially which offer high yield

In this field, you have learned as much as you can depending upon your capability. This is the only way by which you can decide which is the right crop for your hydroponic system. Find out the seeds which are cheap and yield high so that your profit margin is also high.

Explore vitamins b

Many of the beginners in hydroponic gardening ignore the impact of stress on the plants. If you see that your plants are not suffering from any of the diseases then also, they can face stress issues. So, if you think that your plants are facing stress issues offer them vitamin B supplements which are totally safe and with that growth will surge significantly.

These above tips are a basic one, especially for beginners who says that hydroponic gardening is complicated.

Some helpful tips for hydroponic system

- Pay attention to the type of equipment and also focus on the reason for use of these equipment.

- You should know the particular nutrient requirements of your plants.

- There is a need to know the light requirements of your plants.

- Use the hydroponic system that has professional three-part products.

- Try not to use extra additives when you begin; it will make your work quite clumsy.

- Try not to feed your plants haphazardly, feed them with a routine and clear-cut plan.

- You should have all the needed equipment and all the nutrients before you begin.

- Your garden will do well when it is 55*F and sometimes less, you can make the use of AC.

- Ensure that your best light remains in a different room.

- Do a thorough check of your nutrient reservoir daily.

- Reduce the exposure of light to the nutrient solution.

- Have a backup water reservoir that you will use for your change.

- Change the water and the nutrients every two weeks; this should be a complete change.

- The timer you should use should be a digital timer; this will help you control the hark period of the plan.

- Ensure the dark period are dark and nothing interrupts it

- You should clean your system after harvesting a plant and preparing to plant another

- You should quarantine new plants before you add them to the garden. This should be done for about 2 weeks.

- Do not visit your garden after you visit another garden; you should clean up first. This is to prevent the transfer of germs.

- Avoid pets from being in your garden

- You should only visit your garden after you have cleaned up yourself and changed your clothes

Also, you should ensure all your visitors follow the same guidelines

Ensure you have a plan; all the gardening systems are only successful because they have a plan. There is always a need to keep a solid plan. Have a good plan would mean that you will have to know the nutritional requirements of your plant. Also, it means you will have the photoperiods of your hydroponics. What you need to do is to have a week by week feeding plan. This will make you know what to do before the time is upon you to act.

Tips for feeding and nutrients

You should be aware of the nutrient requirements of the plant you want to grow. You should know how strong the nutrient you want to grow going to be. At the initial stage, a lot of plants will need more nitrogen; then, they will begin to need more phosphorus, which is necessary to grow more flowers and fruits. An EC meter will be needed for you to keep proper track of the nutrient that is in your solution.

One thing you should avoid is the act of mixing your plant food; mix your nutrients with the guide at least by this time, you will be able to know what you are mixing. This is also the same if you try to use a nutrient additive.

You have to maintain your nutrient reservoir daily, and the best way to do this is by maintaining two reservoirs; one of the reservoirs will be mixed and ready for use, contain plain water waiting to be mixed. The second reservoir will also make room for you to dechlorinate the water and make it come to room temperature.

Tips for root health

If the root is damaged, then it will be challenging to take up nutrients, and this can lead to damage above the ground. You can protect your roots by allowing the nutrient solution inadequate way, using two hydroponic reservoirs (one of the reservoirs will be plain water for nutrient mix. You can also protect the root by reducing its contact from light. This will reduce the algae and fungus growth, hence prevent root damage.

Chapter 7. Possible Issues of a Hydroponic Garden

Because hydroponic plants can be completely sealed off from the environment by installation in greenhouses, problems with plant pests are much lower than in conventional fields.

Biofilms are another problem—slimy forms of algae, protozoa, and fungi that form quite quickly. These plaques can clog parts of the irrigation system, causing crop failures. Besides, biofilms are an excellent reservoir for bacteria and fungi that can damage the roots of plants.

Algae in hydroponic

Algae can be a problem in any type of hydroponics. In a bubbler system, it often takes place in the nutrient reservoir, especially when the container lets in light. Building up algae reduces the nutrients in the system, which makes the plants work harder as they compete with the algae for food. Algae can also coat the airstone, which is the part of the system that creates the bubbles. The thicker the algae become, the more difficult it is for bubbles to escape, resulting in reduced oxygenation of the water.

Possible diseases and pests in indoor plants

Houseplants with hard leaves are less susceptible to pests, as they cannot easily grip the leaf. Therefore, it is particularly effective in these plants to spray the plant simply with a hard water-steel. In plants such as a sansevieria or the chamaerops humilis, you can occasionally inject with a pressure sprayer now and then as a preventative measure. Specific information on certain pests, vermin species, diseases, or pests can be found here:

Spider Mites

Spider mites are an infection of mites on the plant. Characteristic of the spinnmilde is the small, pear-shaped body, which is about as big as a pinhead. If plants are affected by spider mites, they are deprived of the necessary nutrients.

Variants of the pest

Spider mites are available in many different variations, most of which are plant specific. For example, the common spider mite is common in greenhouses.

Susceptible plants

Plants that are often in dry soil are the most susceptible to an infection of spider mites. Other plants are susceptible depending on the spider mite species. Examples of this are the alocasia and the polyscias.

Place of infestation

Since spider mites often sit under the leaves, they are very small and move little, but they are difficult to discover.

Appearance

Depending on the species, spider mites have a brown, red or yellow-green color and are about 0.3 and 0.5mm in size and have a pear-shaped body. You can best see spider mite infestation on the leaves of plants. Because these get brown, almost coppery points and after a while yellow or brown and fall off.

Reason

Like other mite species, spider mites also become active in warm and dry weather. Often spider mites also occur through old soil. Because of the earth no longer has any nutrients, this is the perfect place for the spider mite to develop. Since even weak plants are frequently attacked, it often helps to repot the plant and thereby give it energy and resistance again.

Distribution

Spider mites benefit from their size and agility. This allows spider mites to reproduce easily through plant-to-plant contact.

Damage to the plant

Sucking nutrients out of the plant, they poke small holes in leaves so plant can no longer absorb or transport nutrients and will die. If the spider mite is not fought well and on time, it becomes a pretty stubborn plague for any plant.

Fighting

Prevention is easier than getting rid of it. Therefore, we recommend occasionally spraying your plants with pesticides. You can prevent infestation by water spraying, as they prefer a dry environment. Do not try to touch the healthy branches with the affected branches. In case of heavy infestation, it is best to use a control agent. The spider mite, in contrast to various louse species, has little resistance to preservatives. Particularly difficult in combating the spider mite is the size of these parasites. These are easy to miss and can then easily spread again. Therefore, the plant should be sprayed thoroughly. Tip: in the evening, spray the plant with water containing 2% yellow soap and 1% spirit. Since the eggs hatch mostly in the evening, this is particularly effective. In addition, you can increase humidity and reduce temperature. Because spider mites love a warm, dry environment.

Scale Ice

Scale lice are often confused with lice. They have an eponymous flat body and are represented in various colors. Scale insects are difficult to control and can cause great damage to the plant.

Variants of the pest

There are two types of scale insects. The boisdubal schildlaus are flat, yellow lice, in which the male is smaller than the female. These are often confused with lice (lice), the lice have a rectangular body. The second species is the oleander schildlaus.

These have an eponymous round shield, which, however, is not in the middle. Due to the color (white or yellow), and the shape of the 2mm pests is often compared with fried eggs.

Susceptible plants

Thyme louse occurs most often in older plants or plants with a woody stem. It is also common in orchids and all types of palm trees.

place of infestation: Both types of scale lice occur on the underside of the leaves as well as in the trunk.

Appearance

In most cases, scale insects live in a group, which together forms a thick crust. Since the male scale insects have a waxy powder, they are often mistaken for woolly lice. Scale insects occur in different colors, including white, gray, or yellow.

Reason

Often the scale louse occurs in a dry air environment. In addition, an abundance of lime in the soil or a poorly groomed plant may be a cause of scale insects.

Distribution

Scale insects spread through insects, birds, or the wind. In indoor plants, they spread by drafts, pets, or contact with clothes.

Damage to the plant

The insect lice attach to the plant and inject a toxic substance into the cells. This substance causes yellow, brown, or red spots on the leaves or flowers. If the pest is not fought, this leads to permanent malformation or even death of the plant.

Fighting

The louse is difficult to fight. Most of the time, there is no alternative but to use chemical means to control. If you do not want to use chemistry, you can also tap the lice with a cotton bud soaked in olive oil. The oil closes the breathing tube of the louse, and the louse will suffocate. Preventive treatment with chemical agents is effective only with repeated use. After contact with scale insects, wash and disinfect your hands carefully to avoid spreading through eggs.

Wollaus

The wolllaus belongs to the family of the louse (pseudococcidae). The name is the typical greasy hairiness of these lice. If it is not treated in time, the lice may spread to all plants.

Variants of the pest

There are several types of lice, of which the citrus louse (planococcus citri) is best known.

Another common species is the long-tailed louse (pseudococcus longispinus). This louse occurs mainly in a humid environment.

Susceptible plants

Woll lice can be found on all indoor plants. However, houseplants such as the more vulnerable are the pineapple, orchid, cactus, passionflower, bromeliad, olive tree, crassula species, and the musa (banana plant) as other species.

Place of infestation

Where exactly lice attack the plant depends on the type of lice. While most lice nest directly on the plant, some species feed on the roots. The wolllaus is one of the few plagues in the world. In the summer months, the birds louse up to 100 eggs, which then hatch within 2 weeks.

Appearance

The lice have a size of 3 to 6 mm and are covered with white, floury discharge from wax wires. They use this layer to protect themselves from the elements and natural enemies. In addition, lay your eggs in this layer.

Reason

Although plants in drafts are more susceptible to woolly louse infestations, the mealybugs have no special requirements for a plant to infect them.

Distribution

Woll lice live in large groups, but they do not spread themselves, but are mostly the people responsible for the distribution over the clothes.

Damage to the plant

The mealybugs feed on phloem. This is the system that provides the plants with nutrients. The lice with their mouthparts suck the phloem out of the leaves, which causes the plant to lose waxing power. In addition, the plant can thereby get yellow or brown leaves and even must be educated. In addition, the hunts honeydew off, which is an optimal place for the formation of shimmer. As the honeydew mixes with the wool-like secretion, the leaf is completely covered. As a result, the plant receives less light, and photosynthesis becomes more difficult.

Fighting

Woll lice are cold-resistant. They can even easily survive temperatures of minus 40 degrees. For the fight, you can mix 12 grams of paraffin oil to one liter of water and spray over the lice. Alternatively, you can do this with alcohol. You must repeat this treatment thoroughly each day to be sure that the fluid has touched all lice. You can also use a pressure sprayer to simply rinse away the lice. In the case of long-term infestation, however, we recommend using chemical control.

Harmfulness to humans

Mealybugs are not harmful to humans.

Special features

Most mealybugs can reproduce both sexually and asexually.

Wool and lice

In dry room air, wool and mealybugs can spread undisturbed:

- Infestation leaves a wooly coating on the stems and leaves

- Oil-containing sprays help, for example with neem oil

- The oil stifles the lice

Black or green lice

The cause of an infestation with black or green lice is often too dry and warm location, especially places above a radiator and in the blazing sun:

- Makes visible by curling the leaves

- Especially young shoots take damage

- Formation of a sticky coating

- Wash off lice with a detergent-based solution

- Change location

Schildlaus

Like the other lice, too dry air promotes the spread of scale insects:

- Brown cusps on the stems and leaves

- Glued leaves that lead to crippling

- Oil-containing sprays are also used here

Healing of infested plants

To slow the spread of the pests, remove as much infected material as possible. Either cut away the infested material completely, or you try to remove the pests with a cloth. After you have come into contact with the vermin, you should disinfect your hands.

Place the plant outside or cover the floor with foils so you can "shower" it off with lukewarm water. This also works preventively. You can use a hard jet of water to simply rinse away most of the plague.

If your infested houseplant is also suitable for outdoors, you can also put it outside to prevent infection of other plants. For example, you can fight the spider mite completely. Make sure, however, that the outside temperature is high enough, and the plant is not in direct sunlight.

If you want to combat the pests with chemicals, multiple treatments are necessary. Therefore, pay close attention to the enclosed instructions for your particular product. After successful treatment, spray the plant with lukewarm rainwater to rinse off the remainder of the chemicals.

Also, clean the planter completely. Take the plant completely out of the pot and remove as much old soil as possible. In addition, check the roots of the plant for your health. Then you can refill the plant pot with new soil.

Chapter 8. Best Plants for Hydroponics

Plants suitable for Hydroculture

Lettuce

Growing salad in hydroponics is elementary, much more than it might seem, even for those who start from scratch and approach the hydroponics world for the first time.

Once you have identified the variety of salad that best suits your needs and tastes, you must obtain the seeds that you will easily find online. Then you will have to buy rock wool cubes (Rockwool) and net jars, a mini-green to store them in the warm, in a protected environment and with net pots, designed precisely for the needs of plants that are grown with hydroponic and aeroponic systems. Therefore, a small hydroponic or aeroponic system will be needed.

One aspect to check - when using rock wool cubes - is the amount of water they absorb, because an excessive amount of liquid could cause the roots to rot and drown them. For this, it is always advisable to check the liquid levels present and possibly wring out the cubes to let out the excess water.

With the right amount of water and the ideal temperature, lettuce seeds will begin to germinate after about 48 hours. When you see the first roots appearing from the rock wool cubes (both from the sides and the base), it means that the time has come to transfer the newly born seedlings to the special mesh pots, which will first be filled with expanded clay and then settled in the hydroponic system you have chosen (or aeroponic). The seedlings inserted in the aeroponic system will then be fed with a special nutrient solution based on water and fertilizers to provide everything they need. It is vital to avoid any fertilizer during the germination phase and then start with a halved dose compared to what is recommended on the package.

Fertilizers for the cultivation of Hydroponic salad

By using suitable fertilizers and in the right dose, the roots of the lettuce seedlings are allowed to develop better and faster than they would use with a traditional cultivation system, also because

- in this way - the roots can receive and assimilate nutrients faster.

To grow the seedlings in a healthy and fast way, thus strengthening their root system to make it more robust, it is possible to opt for some special fertilizers, which contain fundamental substances capable of promoting and increasing growth, accelerating absorption nutrients, and keep the most common salad diseases away. Fertilizers play a central role in the life and health of the plant. Since the hydroponic and aeroponic system does not provide for the presence of fertile soil, to ensure that the salad receives all the nutrients, it is essential to use the right fertilizers to be able to grow plants properly. Strengthening the root system of salad plants and preventing pests means growing healthy, strong, and vigorous plants capable of returning a good harvest.

Hydroponic salad: parameters to monitor

At this point, once the cultivation has started, it is appropriate to keep under control some fundamental values for the health and growth of each plant, such as the pH, which will determine the ability - by the cultivated plant - to correctly absorb the available nutrients.

In order for salad plants to absorb all nutrients correctly, the pH must be slightly acidic, and to ensure that it is always such, it is advisable to often monitor the situation with manual tests. For example, cheap and easy-to-use paper strips for pH testing can be used.

Tips and tricks for a perfect Hydroponic salad

To create a suitable and protected environment, it is recommended to repair and check the salad plants inside a grow box to make them grow well, healthily and faster, without weighing on the cost of the bill.

Among the advantages of using the grow box, there is undoubtedly that of being able to more easily control the temperature than a larger environment and, therefore, less controlled, better manage ventilation, ensure the right lighting (thanks to the reflective mylar sheet present inside the grow box which allows the light to be effectively propagated).

But when will you get your first salad crop?

Much depends on the variety chosen and cultivated, but - in general - it is possible to say that the time required varies between 4 weeks and 80 days. By choosing different varieties and managing the aeroponic system, you can have a fresh, tasty, and healthy salad at any time of the year.

Strawberries

Cross and delight of many professional and amateur growers, the strawberry is a problematic fruit, especially if grown out of season and in unsuitable environments. All difficulties are overcome, especially for those who choose the above-ground cultivation, better known as hydroponic cultivation.

The more than tested technique, especially in strawberry cultivation, offers more than exciting advantages:

- production is standardized;

- there is a considerable saving of energy and water, which is used more rationally;

- production is better in quality and quantity;

- the problem of diseases, molds, and pests that multiply on contact with the ground are entirely forgotten.

Those who choose the hydroponic technique also can produce strawberries in at least two different periods of the year: from October to December and throughout April and May.

If we also take into consideration that once planted, the plants begin to bear fruit after 45 days. It is well understood why this choice is shared by many growers and lovers of indoor cultivation.

Anyone who chooses to switch to this type of technique must first thoroughly wash the roots of their seedlings and insert them in a small pot that contains expanded clay or alchemy of vermiculite and perlite.

It is also essential to have a container that can hold at least 10 liters of water (for each seedling), better if impermeable to the passage of light to avoid the formation of algae and mushrooms.

Among the most popular hydroponic cultivation methods for strawberries, there is the one called NFT hydroponics: to make it simple with this system; it is possible to achieve a good circulation of all the nutrients that the roots need. Everything is automated thanks to the use of a timer that alternates between full and dry moments, essential for the roots to have the right oxygenation.

Obviously, it is essential to have the right fertilizer, which in this case, is composed of nitrogen and potassium and water with the correct pH, which should always be adjusted between 5.5 and 5.6. To make the job easier, there are active acidity regulators on the market.

Finally, you must have the right lighting, and in this case, the lamps for indoor cultivation will be a potent ally.

Once you start your strawberry cultivation, domestic or industrial, it is good to keep in mind that the plant must be regularly pruned: it is wrong not to cut excess leaves, especially before flowering. These will unnecessarily weaken the plant and could favor the creation of mushrooms that are particularly harmful to the future growth of strawberries.

Also, despite the impatience shared by many growers, it is good that the fruit is harvested only when red and ripe, better still if in times of darkness.

Tomatoes

Quality and quantity with Hydroponic tomato cultivation

Tomato is a genuinely functional vegetable in hydroponic culture. It reacts very well to the so-called "soilless cultivation," this because it can easily adapt to different types of substrate and does not require demanding agronomic management.

In tomato hydroponics, multiple substrates can be used:

• Rock wool

• Peat

• Perlite

• Coconut fiber

• Compost

And with all, you can achieve magnificent results. The only precaution that must be paid in the hydroponic cultivation of tomatoes is the temperature. Indeed, excessive maxims could affect the floral drop and, therefore, on the quantity and quality of the product.

Kitchen herbs

The new home dream is to have a thousand and one aromatic herbs on the terrace or the balcony to flavor your dishes with a personal, fresh, and eco-friendly touch. This is why hydroponics has been so successful.

The Greeks already knew it, Francis Bacon spoke about it in 1627 and today hydroponics (literally the art of growing plants in water) is well appreciated in the industrial and domestic field.

The hydroponic cultivation of aromatic herbs has five remarkable qualities:

1. the yield of the product that is developed through indoor cultivation is better;

2. growth is faster;

3. the taste is more intense;

4. the cultivation technique is environmentally sustainable;

5. the water expenditure decreases drastically.

With hydroponic cultivation at home, it is possible to grow any aromatic plant, whether it is parsley, basil, thyme, rosemary, oregano. Still, you can also choose to grow lettuces, tomatoes, strawberries, and who knows what else.

In short, hydroponics allows at reduced costs and with a disarming simplicity to make your terrace or balcony a garden of wonders, a vertical garden, an urban oasis.

Orchids

Orchids lend themselves perfectly to hydroculture. They are, in fact, epiphytic plants (i.e., plants that naturally grow and live on other plants), and humid environments represent their ideal condition for growing well and in health. The plant will develop its roots, which - with the growth and passage of time - will pass through the holes of the pot, to flow directly into the water. Different varieties of orchids can be grown in hydroculture, such as the best-known variety of Phalaenopsis, but also Cattleya, the Dendrobium variety, Paphiopedilum and Oncidium.

One of the main advantages offered by this cultivation technique is represented by the opportunity to supply the plant with a constant quantity of water capable of properly hydrating and irrigating the orchid without damaging it with an excess of liquid. All this - combined with correct fertilization - allows the plant to grow at a much faster rate than traditional cultivation techniques.

Another advantage of orchids grown in hydroculture is given by the typical characteristics of expanded clay, used in these cases instead of the soil or the mix of materials generally used for orchids, which allows faster, easier, and risk-free repotting to damage the roots.

In this way, orchids quickly develop their root system: in a short time, the roots will grow and pass through the holes of the pot in which they are located and will begin to develop directly in the cultivation water.

By doing so, orchid plants will grow faster and healthier, without any disadvantages.

As already mentioned, there are many benefits of using the hydroculture method:

The plant needs much less maintenance

Faster and faster growth

A reduction in the risk of pests and diseases

Greater oxygenation of the roots

Elimination of mold and other allergens.

Chapter 9. Plants to Avoid in Hydroponic Cultivation

Some plants are not precisely indicated in hydroponic cultivation. Here are a few:

Pumpkins

Pumpkins love the sun and well-drained soil with neutral ph.

They are challenging to grow in a hydroponic system as they have large groups of roots that spread rapidly.

Squash

Squash grows at the base of the plant, which means it could rest on damp soils. This will likely encourage mushroom growth.

Also, squash is generally a large plant with minimal yield. There are much better ways to use space in the hydroponic system.

Zucchini

This is a great plant, which means it will need a lot of support. It needs more nutrients than other plants and won't give such a significant yield for space.

It is necessary to keep the temperature around 75 ° F (24 ° C), even during the night. It will also dry out very quickly if it does not have enough water and nutrients.

Potatoes

Most root vegetables are not suitable for hydroponic systems.

The cost of the harvest will be very low compared to the efforts needed to grow it.

Radish

Some plants grow well, but not a good option. You need the right supports to make them grow hydroponically, and in the end, the cost will probably be higher than buying in a store.

Getting the Nutrient Strength Correct

It is important that the nutrient strength is correct as your plants are absorbing their food through the solution. At different stages of growth, they require different nutrient strengths. This one we will focus on getting the nutrient strength correct, which can be confusing to the beginner.

Hydroponics allows you to easily adjust the nutrient solution to give your plants the optimal growing conditions. If the solution is too weak the plant will not grow as quickly as it can and if it is too strong the plant will become ill through overfeeding or looked burned. In the latter cases, you need to just use plain water with no nutrients for a few days to allow the plants to recover and get the excess nutrients out of its system.

If your plants have the optimal nutrient solution, then they will grow like they are on steroids! You will be surprised how quickly they grow when compared to the same plants in soil. Therefore, nutrient strength and mix is absolutely vital for your plants to thrive.

The kit you have bought should come with full information on the nutrient strengths that you require, and it depends on the type of hydroponics system and the growing medium you are using. Check the instructions that came with your kit and follow them for optimal growing conditions.

Setting the Nutrient Strength

In order to set the nutrient strength correctly you will need the following:

1) A chart telling you the nutrient strengths for the plants you are growing and the stage of growth the plant is in.

2) A nutrient strength meters

3) Nutrients and water to adjust the strength of the nutrient solution.

You can get feeding charts for most of the nutrients that you will use, and these have been tested to produce the optimal growing conditions for the plants. Follow this chart as it works and will ensure your plants thrive. Delicate plants like lettuce like a low nutrient strength whereas hardier plants like broccoli which are much greedier require stronger nutrient solutions.

The following table gives you an idea of the nutrient strengths that different plants require. Remember that cF is the feed strength, and the nutrient type is for the plant when it is in the vegetative growth stage or the flowering / fruiting stage (bloom). As some plants don't produce fruits or flowers, they have no need for the bloom nutrient.

Plant	cF level	pH Level	Grow/Bloom Nutrient
Asparagus	14 - 18	6.0 - 6.8	Both
Banana	18 - 22	5.5 – 6.5	Both
Broccoli	28 – 35	6.0 – 6.8	Grow
Cabbage	25 – 30	6.5 – 7.0	Grow
Celery	18 – 24	6.5	Grow
Common Bean	20 – 40	6.0	Both
Cucumbers	17 – 25	5.5	Both
Leek	14 – 18	6.5 – 7.0	Grow
Lettuce	8 – 12	6.0 – 7.0	Grow
Marrow	18 – 24	6.0	Both
Okra	20 – 24	6.5	Both
Pak Choi	15 – 20	7.0	Both
Peppers	18 – 22	6.0 – 6.5	Both

Rhubarb	16 – 20	5.5 – 6.0	Grow
Spinach	18 – 23	6.0 – 7.0	Grow
Strawberries	18 – 22	6.0	Both
Tomatoes	20 – 50	6.0 – 6.5	Both
Zucchini	18 – 24	6.0	Both

For flowers and herbs the following table gives you an idea of the nutrient strengths required:

Plant	cF level	pH Level	Grow/Bloom Nutrient
African Violet	12 – 15	6.0 – 7.0	Both
Basil	10 – 16	5.5 – 6.0	Grow
Carnation	20 – 25	6.0	Both
Ficus	16 – 24	5.5 – 6.0	Both
Parsley	8 – 18	5.5 – 6.0	Grow
Rose	15 – 25	5.5 – 6.0	Both
Sage	10 – 16	5.5 – 6.5	Grow

In order to measure the nutrient strength, you will need a nutrient strength meter and it is worth spending the money to get a good quality one. The three measurements you will take are the cF (conductivity factor), PPM (parts per million), and EC (electrical conductivity). These are pretty much the same thing but using different scales. Some meters will read in only one scale, but the better ones will read in all three, which is better for you as different nutrients may display their requirements in different scales.

Converting between the three is relatively easy. The cF is ten times the EC and the PPM is the EC figure multiplied by either 500 or 700, depending on which PPM scale is being used! Depending on which country you are in and who made your nutrient meter it could be any one or more of these scales that you use.

The first step is to take a reading of the water that you have put in your reservoir (remember to leave it overnight for the chlorine to evaporate away. It will have its own pH level due to containing minerals which can vary from day to day and will vary from area to area. It is, therefore, very important, that you check the pH every time you change the reservoir rather than assuming the water has a certain pH level.

Base nutrients typically come in either one, two or three bottle kids. The single bottle nutrients are not always the best, but they are easy to use. The two bottle sets need equal quantities of both parts added to your reservoir. The three bottle kits are typically a grow, bloom and micro part and the ratio of these three parts will vary during the growth cycle of your plants.

The following table helps you to find the cF or EC for your plants. If your water has a cF of 5 and you need a three-quarter strength nutrient solution, then you are aiming for a cF of about 17. Divide these figures by ten to get the equivalent EC figures.

Water cF	¼ Strength	½ Strength	¾ Strength	Full Strength
1	5	9	13	17
2	6	10	14	18
3	7	11	15	19
4	8	12	16	20
5	9	13	17	21
6	10	14	18	22
7	11	15	19	23
8	12	16	20	24

Add the nutrient required to meet your target cF level. In two or three-part nutrient kits you add the first part, mix it in thoroughly and then add the second part (mixing thoroughly) and finally the third part, again mixing thoroughly. Never mix the parts together all at once as it will interfere in getting accurate reading.

If you go over the required nutrient strength, then simply remove some of the nutrient solution and add some water to dilute the remaining mixture.

Once the cF is correct, check the pH and adjust it appropriately.

Your reservoir water should be changed once every week or two, but you will want to check your nutrient strength as well as your pH every two days as it is likely to vary during that time. Checking every day doesn't give enough time for the system to settle properly and you will end up spending a lot of time trying to balance the system. The levels will do one of three things:

1) Stay the same – the plant is using equal quantities of water and food so just keep the reservoir topped up with nutrient of the same strength.

2) Go down – the plants are using more food than water and you need to top the solution back up to the original strength. It may be that your plants need a stronger nutrient solution as they are using a lot of food. If the leaves are yellowing or showing signs of other deficiencies, then increase the nutrient strength by one or two cF points and see how they are.

3) Go up – this is where the plant uses more water than nutrients which means you need to dilute the nutrient solution with water. It can also mean that you had the nutrient solution too strong to start with, particularly if the leaves were looking burned with brown tips. Lower the cF of the nutrient solution by a few points and observe.

Now this might sound very complex to you but don't worry, you will get the hang of it really quickly. It is nowhere near as difficult as it may sound once you have done it a few times. You will find that very soon this becomes a two-minute check that you can do in your sleep!

Chapter 10. Hydroponics Vs Aquaponics

They sound a lot alike, don't they? Hydroponics and Aquaponics? They are similar in one way, but vastly different where it counts. Hydroponics means, literally, grown in water. If you take the words aquaculture + hydroponics and put them together, you get aquaponics. Let's look at the two processes in more detail to see why one will be better for you over another.

Ditch the soil. Both systems offer growing a garden without soil. This represents a huge benefit. Soil becomes stagnant after years of cultivation, requiring a lot of fertilizer and/or rotation of crops. Simply replacing the soil during repetitive seasons of indoor growth becomes expensive on top of that, soil is easily contaminated with spores or pests laying eggs, perpetuating all of the diseases from one season. Growing in soil almost requires an outdoor garden and living in a climate zone with harsh winters means you can only grow your veggies half of the year. Both systems offer value in growing without soil.

Instead of soil, you'll grow your plants in a biosystem of specially cultured beneficial bacteria, and your very own circle of life will sustain both fish and plants. This healthy substitute for dirt is simple to produce, and you'll wonder why you never tried aquaponic gardening before.

Fertilize the water. Both systems require nutrient-based water for plant growth. Hydroponic gardening employs chemical nutrients, which represents constant overhead. You may obtain your growing medium from any number of suppliers, but let's face it: the uncertain role of chemicals in cancer and birth defects is generating headlines around the world. In aquaponics, you may grow organic vegetables through natural fertilizer produced by fish swimming around the tank. The advantage goes to aquaponics.

Design the right space. Both systems require light and a floor strong enough to withstand some pretty hefty weight. I was clueless. I imagined a sweet little aquarium with plants above it and was shocked to realize a twenty-gallon aquarium weighs a whopping 225 pounds. A concrete floor in the basement sounded smart, but I was hooked on the idea of cute goldfish and had a 14-ft bay window in the dining room, so the scales became my enemy.

Both systems are going to affect your utility bills. The difference between them is that in hydroponics, the water may not be recycled. In aquaponics, the water must be recycled to formulate the rich growth medium to fertilize the plants. A high-water bill would make it cheaper to buy the produce at the market, which makes aquaponics preferable.

Both require a growth medium that serves as an anchor for the plants, helps regulate temperature, and provides constant nourishment. In aquaponics, hydroton is a popular form made from clay. I wanted to get a product I was accustomed to using, but all of them were on the no-no list: sand, vermiculite, peat moss, wood chips, and pearlite. On the plus side, this represented a one-time purchase, and I could live with that. I see no strong value of one system over the other, because both require a mix to hold the plant.

Both systems require an investment in setting up the apparatus. A hydroponic garden is cheaper to start if you employ a wicking or water culture system. Both require a more complex design for some setups, and hydroponics equals the cost of aquaponics when you add a sump pump and additional piping. Aquaponics requires an investment in fish, but the cost will be less than continually buying chemical fertilizers for the water. In this case, the plus goes to aquaponics.

However, the learning curve is definitely higher for aquaponic gardening. Because you are dealing with live organisms to create the fertilizer for your plants, it takes time and experimentation to get the right mix for ideal growth. If you require instant gratification, go with hydroponics. If you like a challenge, like to putter with details, and are willing to wait for results, go with aquaponics. For ease and learning the plus goes to hydroponics.

To better asses these differences, you first have to have a clear idea of how regular gardens work.

Regular gardening:

- Plants are planted on soil, which provides growing medium as well as needed nutrients.

- Sunlight and rain provide other needs for photosynthesis.

- Needed nutrients and water may be supplemented by the use of fertilizers and irrigation.

Hydroponic gardening:

- Plants are placed in inert medium

- Water is constantly pumped through the root for hydration.

- Nutrients are introduced through especially made chemical mixes dissolved in the water.

This system is often seen as more advantageous compared to regular gardening because of the level of control that can be had on the environment. There is also improved hydration and better control over the available nutrients for the plants.

The chemical mixes can be customized according to the needs of specific plants and their current stage in the growth cycle. This translates to yields that are more consistent and enhanced production.

Aquaponic Gardening:

- It is the same with the hydroponic system with regards to the nutrition and hydration of plants. The use of chemical mixes may also be implemented to aid plant growth.

- Fish and bacteria work together to create much, if not all, of the nutrients needed by the plants.

Here, you can see that, although relying solely on fish and bacteria might not give you the exact amount of nutrients that you want, aquaponics is also much more economical.

Chapter 11. Hydroponics Gardening Equipment

It's very fun and rewarding to enter the world of hydroponics, but it can also be daunting. There are so many ways to purchase your hydroponics to make you feel daunting. Although the first machine which appears inexpensive and simple to use can be tempting to purchase, you don't want to end up with equipment that doesn't meet your demands. Here are the main considerations when you are buying your computer.

Flood Chamber

Plants that grow hydroponically either grow in a substratum like a soil that is saturated by nutrient solution or are supported from above and can float without nutrient support. No matter what hydroponic models you want, the nutrient solution needs to be supplied in a flooded chamber. Your flood chamber should be opaque to avoid root damage from light. Hydroponic primitive growers have used aluminum foil-covered fish tanks and masonry pots as well as plastic containers, Styrofoam coolers, and chemical storage bottles.

Nutrient Solution

Because hydroponic plants don't grow in potting soil or another nutrient medium, all the nutrients your plants need to survive must be supplied. Hydroponic solutions include the three most common macronutrients in nitrogen, potassium, and phosphorous fertilizers. The ten minor nutrients are not in fertilizers but that plants still need to survive, are also supplied by hydroponic nutrient solutions. Boron, iron, copper, chloride, molybdenum, manganese, and zinc are nutrients. Hydroponic gardeners starting from the beginning should buy pre-mixed solutions in the nutrient balance. Hydroponic gardeners who have more experience, can choose to blend their nutrient solutions to give their crop a custom nutrient balance.

pH Testing Kit

The pH of the solution is lowered and made more acidic so that the plants are less able to absorb nutrients from the solution. When the pH of the solution decreases and is acidic, the solution. This can be avoided by modifying the solution until it gets too acidic or by adding alkaline substances. The pH of the answer must be periodically checked with a pH check kit. Local pharmacies sell pH test strips. Or you can visit a pool supplies store to purchase a liquid test kit.

Lighting

The majority of hydroponic systems are built indoors under carefully regulated lighting conditions. You will get some natural light for your plants if you use hydroponics in a greenhouse. But you may want to incorporate artificial light for short days, even in natural light conditions. A combination of crisp white fluorescent bulbs and plant lights is a great artificial light for hydroponic gardening. This mixture provides the right number of red and blue light waves to develop with your plant. One of growing of the fluorescent lights under which your plants grow should be included. The plants should be put to not exceed 12 inches from the fires.

Coconut Coir

Coconut coir is a naturally occurring byproduct of cocoa processes irrespective of the hydroponic market. The outer husk of a coconut consists of fibers widely used to manufacture several things from floor mattresses to pins. The dust and short fibers are combined to produce coir after the long fibers are used for this purpose. The coconuts consume high nutrient concentrations during their life cycle, while the coir has to undergo the maturation process before it becomes a viable medium for development. Contaminated water is a by-product of this process, as 300 to 600 liters of water are required per cubic meter of coir. However, this maturation can take up to six months, and a report suggests that the working conditions are unsafe and unlawful in North America and Europe during the maturation period. While coconut coir has terrific material properties, given the fact that it needs care, health risks, and environmental impacts. The dark, brittle, chunky, and fibrous material is exposed to water and grows about three-four times its original size. Combined with its capacity to retain water and resistance to pests and diseases, this feature makes it an effective medium for growth. Coconut coir, also referred to as coir peat, provides engineered conditions for growth as an alternative to Rockwool.

Rice husks

Parboiled rice husks (PBH) are a farm byproduct that otherwise would not be commonly used. Over time they decay, require drainage, and retain even less water than stones. The effects of crop growth regulators were shown by a study that rice husks do not affect.

Perlite

A volcanic rock overheated in very light extended glass caves. It is loosely used in the bath or is used in plastic sleepings. It is also used to decrease soil density in potting mixtures

Vermiculite

Vermiculite, much like perlite, is a mineral that is overheated until it expands into light gallstones. Vermiculite has more water than perlite and a natural wicking feature, and in a passive hydroponic system will draw water and nutrients. If the plant roots are surrounded by too much water and too little air, the water retention potential of the medium can be decreased slowly by mixing an amount of perlite.

Pumice stone

One of the essential tools used in hydroponics. Like perlite, pumice is a thin, mined volcanic rock used in hydroponics.

Sand

Sand is available cheaply and easily. It is durable, however, not retaining water very well, and has to be sterilized between applications. Since the sand is easy to reach, and sand shortages are in demand, we are on the horizon as we run out.

Gravel

The same type used in aquariums, but if any small gravel is first washed, it can be used. The plants that cultivate in a traditional, modern gravel filter bed are indeed grown with gravel hydroponics, and water is circulated through the electric powerhead pumps. Gravel is cheap, easy to maintain, drains well, and won't be filled with water. However, it is secure, and the roots of the plant will dry up if the system does not supply continuous water.

Wood fiber

Wood fiber is a highly efficient organic substitute for hydroponics derived from steam wood friction. It profits from the very long preservation of its foundation. Since the earliest times of hydroponics science, wood wool (e.g., wood slivers) has been applied. However, most recent work has shown that wood fibers can adversely influence 'plant growth control' regulators.

Sheep wool

Wool from shearing sheep is a limited but promising medium for sustainable production. The use of sheep wool has led to higher output from the substrate being tested and improvement of productions in all substrates with a biostimulator made of lactic acid, humic acid, and Bacillus subtilis.

Rock wool

The most popular medium in hydroponics is rock fiber (mineral fiber). Rock wool is an inert substrate for operating and recycling systems. Rock wool is a moth material, basalt, or 'slag,' which is spun into a single fiber bundle and is bound to a capillary medium and is effectively secured against the most prevalent microbiological degradation.

Rock wool is usually only used for seedling or with newly cut clones but can remain for life on the plant basis. The advantages and drawbacks of rock wool are numerous. The latter is the potential (mechanical) skin irritation during handling (1:1000). Coldwater flushing provides typically relief. The proven efficacy as a commercial hydroponic substratum includes the advantages. The bulk of rock wool marketed to date is a non-hazardous, non-carcinogenic commodity covering the type of labeling and labeling (CLP) in Note Q of the European Union.

Mineral wool

These products can be designed to support a large amount of water and air, which support the root growth and the absorption of nutrients in hydroponics and provide an excellent mechanical structure that stabilizes the plant by their fibrous nature. The apparent pH of mineral wool makes them unsuitable for plant growth initially and needs "conditioning" to produce a wool with a sufficient, stable ph.

Brick shards

Brick shards have gravel-like characteristics. The inconvenience of altering the pH and needing additional cleaning before reuse is also added.

Polystyrene packing peanuts

Packing polystyrene peanuts are inexpensive, readily available, and have good drainage. We may, however, be too light for other applications. They are primarily used in tube-closure systems. Please note that polystyrene peanuts must be non-biodegradable, and biodegradable packaging peanuts are broken into a sludge. Styrene can be ingested and passed on to the customers; it is a potential concern for safety.

Except for these tools, some considerable non-physical types of equipment include:

Your Available Space

Where are you going to cultivate your plants exactly? In your backyard, a small greenhouse? A big wardrobe? Your cellar? Once you buy your supplies, make sure you measure the square images of the area you use to see exactly how many hydroponics are available. Try to create a gap of at least a meter between each row to easily reach your garden if you intend on growing rows of plants.

The idea about Your Plants

You probably already have an idea of what hydroponics you want to develop. You now have to make sure that you use hydroponics to enable those plants to grow. If your plants have more prominent, thicker roots, you do not want to buy thin, shallow trays. So if you're going to only grow smaller plants, you won't waste your money on a variety of eighteen-inch containers. Speak to your retailer of hydroponics about the method, medium, and fertilizer that best fits your plant size and growth rate. Many manufacturers also have telephone numbers, which allow you to discuss this form of those problems with hydroponic professionals.

Your Budget

You will decide how much money you want to invest and seek to make maximum use of this budget before purchasing your hydroponic equipment. However, start-up costs mustn't be the only hydroponic expenditure. You also need to seek to calculate the energy that your light requires and how often your equipment will be replaced. It will save you a lot of money to spend a little more when you finally purchase the unit if you intend to maintain your hydroponics system for years.

Your Time

You certainly don't want to spend all of your time cultivating seedlings like most hobby growers. That is why you can always take into account just how workers-intensive processes are.

Anything such as an aircraft system could sound attractive instantly. However, since something which goes wrong with the timer will cause the roots to dry very quickly, these systems often have to be more cautious than the rest. The luxury of rustling from job to home to save your plants in case of power failure is not open to most people. Look for a system that provides a broader margin of error, such as a medium that can accommodate a lot of air and water.

The pH is dependent on temperature, so look for an automatically compensated pH meter (ATC). If tested at various temperatures, the pH-reading of your nutrient solution would be various, making it difficult to achieve an accurate, repeatable measurement.

You need to calibrate your pH meter, as it will drift. When you purchase your pH meter, make sure that you buy some calibration solutions and follow the instructions of the company for testing and calibration of your meter.

Phosphoric acid to decrease pH and potassium hydroxide to improve pH may be used to change the pH of your nutrient solution. These substances can be harmful at high concentrations, but they are fairly safe. Most individuals tend to purchase pH-adjustors that are easy to use from a variety of different suppliers, such as pH-up and pH down products from General Hydroponic.

Chapter 12. Micronutrients, Liquid Nutrients and Dry Nutrients

Micronutrients

Micronutrients are only needed in small quantities. But they are essential for plant growth. These include:

•Chlorine (CI)

•Copper (Cu)

•Manganese (Mn)

•Boron (B)

•Iron (Fe)

•Molybdenum (Mo)

•Zinc (Zn)

There are also other nutrients that plants extract in much smaller quantities. They are rarely in pre-made plant foods, but still have a range of considerable effects on a plant's living processes.

Calcium (Ca): Cell wall creation. Too little stunts growth.

Sulfur (S): Protein synthesis.

Iron (Fe): Chlorophyll development and sugar creation.

Magnesium (Mg): Chlorophyll and enzyme creation. Too little causes yellowing of leaves.

Boron (B): Combines with calcium for cell wall creation. Too little causes week stems.

Manganese (Mn): Creation of oxygen in photosynthesis. Too little causes yellowing of leaves.

Zinc (Zn): Respiration, chlorophyll, and nitrogen metabolism. A deficiency results in small leaves.

Copper (Cu): Enzyme activation; respiration and photosynthesis. A deficiency results in pale and yellow leaves.

Selecting Your Hydroponic Nutrient

Beginner: pre-made nutrient solutions

N-P-K only makes up a part of the solution, with the rest comprising of filler and other nutrients that fuel the growth process. It's vital to remember that you can't use nutrient solutions that are designed for soil use. At first, it's best to search for a solution that is effective at growing a variety of crops. The correct concentration for the solution is crucial as the plants depend on what is mixed into the water that circulates around the system. That said, you'll easily find pre-made solutions with mixing instructions that correspond to your plants and the conditions that you're growing in. This makes things simple if you don't want the extra work of creating your own solutions. A warning - ensure that the packaging explicitly mentions that the nutrient solution is specifically designed for hydroponic practice.

Advanced: mixing your own nutrient solutions

More advanced hydroponic growers often wish to mix their own solutions to suit the type of plants they're growing. In order to do this, you will need to obtain the correct salts and dissolve them according to the following instructions. The following mixes create 1 gallon of nutrient solution, but these can be multiplied to suit your needs. For best results, it's important to try to get hold of high-quality raw materials. As for the mixing process, fill a container with water warm enough to dissolve salt, and then proceed to dissolving each salt in the outlined quantities. It's best to add and dissolve each salt one at a time.

Nutrient Solution for Vegetable Crops (1 Gallon):

Calcium Nitrate (Ca $(NO_3)_2$): 6 grams

Potassium Nitrate (KNO_3): 2.09 grams

Sulfate of Potash (K_2SO_4): 0.46 grams

Monopotassium Phosphate (KH_2PO_4): 1.39 grams

Magnesium Sulfate ($MgSO_4$): 2.42 grams

7% Fe Chelated Trace Elements: 0.40 grams

Nutrient Solution for Fruit Crops (1 Gallon):

Calcium Nitrate (Ca $(NO_3)_2$): 8 grams

Potassium Nitrate (KNO_3): 2.80 grams

Sulfate of Potash (K_2SO_4): 1.70 grams

Monopotassium Phosphate (KH2PO4): 1.39 grams

Magnesium Sulfate (MgSO4): 2.40 grams

7% Fe Chelated Trace Elements: 0.40 grams

Nutrient Solution for Flowering Crops (1 Gallon):

Calcium Nitrate (Ca (NO3)2): 4.10 grams

Potassium Nitrate (KNO3): 0.46 grams

Sulfate of Potash (K2SO4): 1.39 grams

Monopotassium Phosphate (KH2PO4): 1.39 grams

Magnesium Sulfate (MgSO4): 2.40 grams

7% Fe Chelated Trace Elements: 0.40 grams

n. b. The Chelated Trace Element needs to be made up of:

Iron - 7%

Manganese - 2%

Zinc - 0.40%

Copper - 0.10%

Boron - 1.30%

Molybdenum 0.06%

I wish you the best of luck when making your own nutrient solution for the first time! Remember to wait for the solution to cool down before using it within your system.

Managing Varying Concentration and pH Levels

Over time the nutrient solution that you use will change in terms of concentration and pH level. I recommend that you use a digital Parts Per Million (PPM) meter that measures the concentration of salts in your solution. You can then compare the PPM concentration and continuously re-measure in order to keep the concentration of your solution as consistent as possible. This ensures your plant is able to continue extracting what it requires. The pH level of the solution also impacts a plants ability to absorb nutrients. An optimal pH level for plants is generally between 6.0 and 6.5, and to achieve this consistently you can utilize a readily available and affordable pH test and control kit. Easy to follow instructions will be provided with all kits.

By taking the time and effort to carefully control the concentration and pH levels of your nutrient solutions, you will reap the benefits of having plants that grow more consistently and predictably.

Controlling Water Microbes

Another obstacle with keeping your nutrient solution effective is ensuring that the water remains sterile. Harmful anaerobic microbes can occur in your water which offsets the chemical/biological equilibrium in your nutrient solution - this can cause damage to the root systems of your plants. These microbes are likely to appear when water is warm and still and will be evident from bad smells and brown roots.

To best prevent bad microbes, I recommend maintaining the water's temperature between 68-75 degrees Fahrenheit, along with using a pump to regularly move the water around your system. This promotes oxygen and in turn good bacteria (aerobic microbes) that can fend off the bad anaerobic microbes. In order to monitor and regulate the temperature of the water in your solution, I simply suggest using an inexpensive aquarium thermometer.

Now that we've covered how to develop nutrient solutions to promote optimal plant growth, you will now be learning the importance of lighting for the growth of your plants and how you can create efficient lighting for your hydroponic configuration.

Liquid Nutrients

Let's start with a liquid solution that most beginners use. These are the general hydroponics flora series.

Basic Applications Table	FloraGro		FloraMicro		FloraBloom	
	tsp/gallon	ml/100 liters	tsp/gallon	ml/100 liters	tsp/gallon	ml/100 liters
Cuttings and Seedlings	1/4	33	1/4	33	1/4	33
General Purpose - Mild Vegetative	1	132	1	132	1	132
Aggressive Vegetative Growth	3	396	2	264	1	132
Transition to Bloom	2	264	2	264	2	264
Blooming and Ripening	1	132	2	264	3	396

Label of the flora series

We must look at the basic applications table. If you are growing leafy greens, you need to use the 'general purpose – mild vegetative' nutrient mix.

If you are growing tomatoes, you first must use the 'general purpose – mild vegetative' mix. This is to encourage foliage growth. When the plant produces flowers, you need to switch to the 'blooming and ripening' nutrient blend.

How to mix liquid nutrients

Take water from your tap, rainwater, or distilled water and use a TDS meter to give you the amount of total dissolved solids in your water. Tap water should be around 100-400ppm while distilled water is less than 25ppm.

You need to know how much water you are going to use. Knowing the amount of water you have will be crucial to the dosing of the nutrients. This is how I mix my nutrients with the flora series:

1.I fill a 5-gallon bucket with tap water and let it sit overnight to air out the chlorine.

2.I read the PPM of my tap water with a TDS meter and see it has 350PPM.

3.I am growing lettuce, and my seeds have already been started. I am ready to transplant them to my system. In this case, I must choose the general-purpose – mild vegetative option.

4.From the basic application table, I see that I need one teaspoon (five grams) per gallon (three point seven liters) of water for the flora gro, micro, and bloom.

5.I add five teaspoons (twenty-five grams) of flora gro into the bucket and stir with a stirring stick until it has dissolved. I use five teaspoons because my solution is five gallons (eighteen liters).

6.I add five teaspoons of flora micro into the bucket and stir until it is dissolved.

7.Lastly, I add five teaspoons of flora bloom to the five-gallon bucket and stir until it has dissolved.

8.After the nutrients are added, I measure the pH of the water. Most likely, the pH will be too high. You need to add a pH down solution to bring the pH between six and six and a half. You cannot add the pH down solution straight into the bucket. This will cause the nutrients to dissipate out of solution.

What you need to do is to take a cup and fill it with water from the nutrient solution. Add some pH down solution to the cup and mix it with the water in the cup. Once the pH down solution is mixed with the nutrients in the cup, pour it into the five-gallon reservoir. Measure the pH of your five-gallon mix and repeat until the pH is 6.5.

9.As a final check, I will test the TDS of the solution, and I should measure around 1000ppm + the initial reading that we took at the beginning. My TDS reading will tell me I have 1350PPM (1000PPM nutrient solution + 350PPM from my water source).

The reason for using a separate cup with the pH down solution is that it is a strong acid that can make the nutrients dissipate out of the solution. This can be seen if white crystals are forming in the nutrient mix.

Dry Nutrients

A 3-part powder nutrient solution from Master blend

Dry nutrient mixing consists of three parts. This is a mix that is widely used in the hydroponics community. Other mixes like the master blend or any other three-part nutrient powder mix are similar in use.

Calcium nitrate

How to mix a dry solution

The seller of the solutions will have guidelines for the mixing ratio. If we look at the website of hydro-gardens, we see they have a table that displays all we need to know.

Mixing instructions for chem-gro lettuce formula

Nutrient mix for five gallons (eighteen liters) of water in grams:

N-P-K: 8-15-35: 8 oz.=227 grams/20= 11.35 grams/5 gallons

Calcium nitrate: 8 oz.=227 grams/20= 11.35 grams/5 gallons

Magnesium Sulfate: 5 oz.=142 grams/20= 7.1 grams/5 gallons

This is a step by step guide on how to prepare dry nutrients:

1.Clean the residue of the previous batch.

2.Know the volume of your mixing container.

3.Fill the tank with water. Low ppm water is preferred. Do not exceed 70°F (21°C).

4.Use a stirring stick or submersible pump to move the water in a stirring motion. Measure the TDS of the base water.

5.Weigh out the correct amount of each part and put them into separate cups. For one hundred gallons, you need eight ounces of the 8-15-36 main nutrient mix, eight ounces of calcium nitrate, and five ounces of magnesium sulfate.

6.Put the powder in the solution one by one. Start with solution A and add the part when solution A is completely dissolved. Do this until you have all three parts dissolved. Use a bucket with warm water (max 70°F or 21°C) to dissolve the Calcium nitrate (part C). When the calcium is dissolved in the warm water, pour it in the nutrient mix.

7.Measure the pH of the water and bring it down to 6 to 6.5 if need be. Use the same pH down method as I described with the liquid nutrients.

8.Check the TDS of the water. It should be around 1575ppm + the TDS you started with (source water).

Conclusion

We have now covered most of the important bases when it comes to the particular dos and don'ts of hydroponic gardening and while there is still so much that can be shared, this is definitely going to be a hobby that will keep you learning as you go. As a means of trying to pull all of this together and to summarize what you mainly need to focus on, this would really be the following: The type of plant or plants that you are wanting to grow in the climate that you have available to you. Remember to choose your system to best meet the needs of the plants that you are wanting to grow, the space that you have available, the best possible method to be making use of and trying to get all of this to operate within your budget.

Over the course of setting up your system, fine tuning it and dealing with all of the little tweaks and corrections, make sure that you pay special care and attention to what your plants are telling you all the time. I would highly recommend that you check the pH of your water and nutrient solution on a daily basis. I would pay special attention to getting your nutrient solution correct so that your plants can get all of the right nutrients from the time that you set up your system. By doing it this way, you will be less likely to be wasting money on having to replace plants that are under stress or become diseased.

Make sure that when you are using pumps and timers that these are in proper working order all the time - this will also save you thousands in the long run. I would also highly recommend that you have a plan in place for any system failures, especially things like power failures. Do you have a back-up system or plan in place that will at least protect your plants, even for a short while until you can get your actual system back up and running once again. And check on your system very regularly so that you will be able to pick up on any diseases or system problems as soon as possible. This makes it somewhat easier to address and fix before it affects all of the plants.

Hydroponics is spreading around the world and such systems offer many new alternatives and opportunities for producers and consumers to make high-quality productions, including vegetables enriched with bioactive compounds. This has provided a general overview of the role of hydroponics in improving these important types of non-essential nutrients, and based on the above discussion, hydroponics appears to be an essential tool for providing high-quality vegetables. Hydroponic and soil-based production systems, however, require good control and must be implemented correctly, taking full account of the needs of plants, soil, water, the environment, producers and consumer safety.

You see, hydroponics is not only about being able to become self-sufficient and self-reliant in growing your own food and vegetables, your little garden is also highly likely to provide you with a tremendous sense of pride and accomplishment. Imagine how incredible you will feel the first time that you are able to pick and enjoy your first cherry tomatoes and Buttercrunch lettuce to enjoy over a family dinner.

CPSIA information can be obtained
at www.ICGtesting.com
Printed in the USA
LVHW020311230221
679613LV00008B/495